BATTLING DEPRESSION

Winning the War in our Minds

D1736135

RUSSELL BUTLER

Dream Loud Publishing

Printed in the United States of America

ISBN-13: 978-1940816074

ISBN-10: 1940816076

Dedicated to Robert Heath Stewart
1981-2008

CHAPTER ONE

A Happy Home

MY NAME IS Russell Butler. I want to share my story with you. If it helps to save the life of one person from suicide, I will have done what I was called to do.

I am thirty-three years old. I'm sure you're thinking, "Thirty-three? This guy is not that old." But the fact that I am alive to tell you my story at thirty-three is nothing short of a miracle.

I was born in Lubbock, Texas, October 25, 1981, to Joe and Cathy Butler—two of the best parents in the world, I might add. I have two older brothers, Corey and Rob. We grew up in your typical middle class family. My dad worked on the railroad for seventeen years, and after that drove a truck until the day he retired. My dad was always the hardest-working man I knew, and quite honestly is my hero. My dad also has one of the sweetest spirits of any man

I know. I remember, even after a 14-hour day in a truck, he still made time to teach me how to throw a curveball. He would be my catcher in the back yard for hours, and always took an interest in his boys' lives. He looked forward to coming home and hearing about our eventful days, and he loved summer nights at the baseball field.

I remember vividly at the age of twelve pitching in a very important game. This game meant a championship, and our moving on to Dallas for the state all-star title. It was a very close game, but it was nearing the end, and dad still wasn't there. Every time I got up on the mound I would look to find him. Every time I stepped into the batter's box, I would look around and hope that maybe he would be standing there by my mom. I knew he had to work, but there was still a tiny hope I would look up and see him somewhere in the stands. In the second to last inning, I heard the honk from a diesel truck in the distance and I saw my dad pulling up into the parking lot!

I'll never forget the joy that rushed through me and how proud I was to see my dad standing out there as I closed out the game. Those last couple of innings, I threw harder, ran faster, and did everything I could to make my daddy proud. I knew I didn't have to do anything special to please him, because he was proud of us boys no matter what. Still, I wanted to prove something to him. I glanced at him from the dugout, and he would give me a smile and a big thumbs up. We went on to win the game, but unfortunately didn't make it past the first round in Dallas. For as long as I live, I will never forget my daddy pulling up in center field to watch his boy play his heart out.

He didn't have to show up after such a hard day, but he did. He was there. My dad always made it a priority to be there for us. We never had much, but we *never* did without love. From the time I was born until this very day, my dad tries his very best to make sure we are taken care of. Even if he doesn't have the money, if he knows any of his boys are hurting, he will give all he has. That is my dad. The hardest working and most loving man I know.

Speaking of love, let's talk about the most loving, caring, beautiful woman a man could ask for, my mama. She is the woman who showed love even in the hardest of times, when we did not deserve love. My mom was a stay-at-home mom, which is pretty rare these days. She showed my brothers and me the kind of love every boy dreams of from a mama. Like dad, mom was always there for everything - the bumps, the bruises, the good times, the bad times, the laughs, the tears, the wants, the fears.

When I think about my mom, a picture stands out in my mind. I was six, Corey was twelve, and my big brother Rob was eighteen. We all came down with the chicken pox at the same time that year. The picture shows me on my mama's back, and Corey and Rob hugging mom, as we stood in the kitchen covered in chicken pox. This picture encapsulates my mom. Even when the load was heavy, she carried it with grace and courage.

My mom never missed school events or sports games. Even though she didn't quite understand baseball, she cheered as loud as she possibly could. My mom brought us boys up in Bethany Baptist Church, where we rarely missed a Sunday. After church we would come home as a family and sit at the dinner table ready to partake in the feast she made from scratch. I can still remember the smell of the chicken fried steak, mashed potatoes, and cream gravy. I can taste her sweet tea and hear the laughs we shared at the table. We would talk about everything, from the Bible verses I learned that day and the sermon to what we had coming up for the week.

Mom would always eagerly help with any homework we needed to get done. Our home was always one filled with joy, peace, and love, and my mama made sure of that. On top of cooking, cleaning, and helping us boys with school, mom was an awesome seamstress. We always wanted the latest designer clothes, but we didn't have the money to buy them. So mom did everything she could to make what we had look identical to the brand name clothing. The best fashion trick she ever pulled off for me was an M.C Hammer outfit that rocked from head to toe. She made the gold vest with the black shirt underneath and of course the best parachute pants ever. Can't touch that!

My parents may not have always been perfect, but they are the people who would give anyone the shirts off of their backs. Growing up I remember my brother Rob having a few friends come to live with us when those friends were having tough times in their own homes. The same welcome was offered to Corey's friend, Bruce, and eventually one of my best friends, Michael. Our house was always filled with as many people as we could pack in, from baseball teams to church groups to my oldest brother's rock band. This was our home, and our door was always open. I have friends to this day who still talk about "the good old days" at the Butler house. Everyone was incredibly blessed by my parents' hospitality – especially me as a loved son.

CHAPTER TWO

Lead Me To The Cross

I **WAS EIGHT YEARS** old the day my mama asked me, "Do you want Jesus to come live in your heart?" I recall the moment we hit our knees in the living room in front of our old couch and I gave my life to Jesus Christ. I'm not sure I fully knew what that whole action meant, but I know that my God did--He accepted that eight-year-old me into his Kingdom, and I felt it. I went to school the very next day and told all my friends, "Jesus lives in my heart!" Oh, the faith of a child. What a remarkable thing.

From that moment on, I knew I was a Christian and that I had a calling to do special things in this life. I never knew exactly what that calling was, but I always felt the urge to help others. Like everyone in this world, I'm far from perfect. All I knew then was God loved me and would never reject me. I accepted His mission to show people that very same love.

As the years went on, the faith of my family was tested. My dad lost jobs here and there for various reasons and I remember having to move quite a few times before I hit high school. One day in third grade, I came home from school to discover all our belongings packed up and ready to go. My dad had suddenly lost his job, and we were relocating to Sweetwater, TX. You can only imagine how devastated I was leaving behind all of my close childhood friends and going to this unknown place.

Every day in Sweetwater, Corey and I would come home from school and complain to mom and dad. I know this didn't make their lives any easier. Seeing their kids unhappy and having a hard time weighed on my parents more than I could have ever known. Corey and I did make some friends here and there, but Sweetwater still wasn't home. We felt displaced from where we felt most happy, and we let it show.

After months of our grumbling, my dad decided to look for more work in Lubbock, and it wasn't long before we were headed back. There was a slight problem, though. We had nowhere to live and very little money. We drove into Lubbock late at night, with everything packed in our old Buick, including our dogs. When we arrived, my mom got on the phone with my Aunt Barbara and asked if we could stay with her for a while. Barbara was happy to house us, so that's where we headed. We stayed with Barbara's family for a while, and after a few months (plus a little family feud) we were on to the next place. I recall we were driving around aimlessly with nowhere to go when we stopped at a pay phone.

My mom got out of the Buick, took a chance, and called an old church friend, Quepha Bolt. It was the night before Easter and the only reason I remember this fact is my older brother Corey said, "Most people are getting ready to hunt Easter eggs, and we are hunting for a place to live." At that moment, our dog Timmy let out a loud snort and brought a much-needed bit of comic relief to our current situation. Things were tough no doubt. But laughter can shift the weight of any situation.

Quepha responded and told my mom "our door is always open." Such true

Christianity and such beautiful hospitality once again. Quepha has been this kind of open and giving friend to my family since I can remember, and she has never let us down. She has always seen needs and has always met them, which is how true love is best expressed.

After a few days of living with Quepha's family, we were in dire need of groceries but we didn't let on. My mom waited and waited to go to the store because money was so tight. Finally the day came when Quepha noticed our struggles and she told my mom, "Get up. Let's go to the store." Mom told me she remembers being so embarrassed because she knew we didn't have the money to get groceries. When they got to the store, mom walked with Quepha quietly. Quepha noticed my mom wasn't putting anything in the basket, and said, "You'd better tell me what you and the boys want, or I'll just pick it out myself." She has always been one of the kindest souls I know, and the same goes for the entire family. I remember sleeping on a mattress in the floor of their home, praying and crying, "I want our own home." God bless that family, because they made their home ours.

After several years of financial struggle, my dad landed a pretty good paying job, and we moved into a house where I spent my junior high school years. Like with most kids at this age, this is when acceptance is everything. I did what came naturally and gravitated towards athletics. Call it the law of attraction, or God's divine plan, but the people from that season all came into my life for a very special purpose. We challenged each other even at thirteen to be the best we could be, and we still hold each other accountable today.

I'll never forget the first time I met one of my best friends, Alan Roa. We were at our first pep rally in seventh grade, and neither one of us were sure what "crowd" to interact with. I remember making eye contact with him, and he kind of gave me a nod to come and sit by him. We instantly became friends. Alan always talked about "knowing someone before you know someone." I knew exactly what that meant, because I feel the same way.

They say the eyes are the windows to the soul, and I feel there is validity to that. Turns out Alan and I would share several classes together and were both running backs in football. At our first football practice, coaches had all the running backs get together and run drills. It was during this time another friend from elementary school, Ben Flores, came back into my life. Alan, Ben, and I were by each other's side through thick and thin in those years. We shared many classes, got into trouble, and played every sport together. Sports became the common denominator for meeting all of my best friends. All of us would ride an old "yellow dog" bus to rival junior high schools and prepare for battle. My best friend Michael happened to be at one of our rival junior highs, and we would face off on many occasions.

Michael and I met in kindergarten. His home was my second home, and vice versa. Growing up, Michael was like my third brother. He also had two older brothers, which made both of us the" babies" of our families. I remember his staying with us for weeks at a time in during the summer. I was such a mama's boy, I was too afraid to stay away from home up until junior high. During junior high and high school the dots started connecting. God brought these guys into my life at this time, along with Lance Cantu, Jeremy Thiel, Zac Hughes, Rhys Heinsch, Skyler May, Michael Salazar, Roger Ruiz, Micah Cantu, and Heath Stewart.

Remember the name Heath Stewart. He is the inspiration for this book.

CHAPTER THREE

Innocence Lost

JUNIOR HIGH IS a little bit of a blur, and I had many learning experiences, but I could not wait for high school. To me high school meant freedom. We would soon have our licenses, off-campus lunches, prom, homecoming, and it was all so exciting.

It was the first day of sophomore year for us at Monterey High School. I recall this being one of the most exciting days of my life. I woke up earlier than normal to press my jeans and bright yellow polo shirt. I had saved up a little money over the summer to get the latest pair of Michael Jordan shoes and had gotten a fresh haircut the day before. I was ready for high school, or so I thought I was. We all arrived at school a little early to see each other's schedules and whether we had any matching classes. As we passed each other in the hall we would give a fist bump and ask your typical high school questions: "How bad was that class?" " Where are we going for lunch?" and most important, "Did you see that girl?" The end of our school day was our favorite part: football for them and baseball for me. I had many friends and coaches upset because I made the choice to specialize in baseball and play it year round. My dream was to play professional baseball, so I felt that was a choice I needed to make.

School and sports aside, let's dive a little deeper into my relationships with these guys. We did everything together. Alan once put it into words the best way I know how. There is a part in the movie *Good Will Hunting* during which Robin Williams is describing Matt Damon's character's love for his friends. He says that any one of them would take a bat to someone's head for the other—that's called loyalty. When it comes to our friendships, you never have to ask why, or where, or when. You just be there for them, for whatever they are going through.

One of my most memorable classes was Algebra I. This is not because I HATE math or that my teacher was a little

strange but because I had two of my boys
in that class. Heath, Alan, and I all sat
in the same row. I'm not sure why, but
our teacher never separated us, and this
probably contributed to the fact I am awful
at math. While she would try her best to
teach us negative-fifteen-plus-eight-minus-
eight-and-two-thirds, we talked about
the weekend and our girl problems. You
know, at sixteen years old these are major
problems! Ha. Regardless of how big or
small our so-called problems were, we
were learning daily how to deal with life
choices—and hoping we were making the
best of them. Through our seemingly minor
conversations, this is where we developed
a bond only few are blessed to have in this
lifetime. These conversations happened
more and more as we went on through
our high school years. It's amazing to
think about nights after a football game or
around a bonfire talking about life. Where
did we fit in the grand scheme of life? Who
is God to us? Am I on the right track? After
some "deep" discussion we would go back
to drinking beer and punching each other
as hard as we could.

The beautiful thing about all of my

friends is how amazingly talented they are in their own unique ways. Alan is smart and witty, Lance is the stud athlete, and then there's Heath: the golden boy. We all ha d our own little qualities that made us individuals, but I remember Heath having it all. None of us were above any social group, and we mingled with everyone. If you watched Heath, though, he embodied this quality. As soon as you met Heath, he would make you feel loved by his amazing smile. He would look you in the eye, shake your hand and make you feel as if you had known him all your life. Heath served on our student council, maintained one of the highest GPAs of our class, played quarterback and was one hell of a baseball player. Aside from all of that, he was always the one we went to for advice. He truly listened to you about any and everything you were going through. If he didn't have an answer, which he usually always did, he would always tell you, "you're in my prayers, bro." And he meant it. He would always make it a point to ask how the situation was going and if there was any progress. Heath was what you call "a man's man." Every guy in the school knew who he was and respected him, and most every girl wanted to date him.

As high school went on, so did the good times and partying. We worked hard and played even harder. Alcohol was usually always in the picture for all of us during the weekend, and I have always been one to try anything once. That being said, I tried pot for the first time when I was 14, and alcohol came into the picture in high school. During this time I was still focused more on baseball to really get into anything stronger than weed. As the years went on, however, I was always curious. I had people offer me mushrooms, cocaine, ecstasy, and an assortment of many drugs throughout high school. This is when the spiritual warfare began.

To add to that spiritual warfare, some of my grades were slipping, and things were not always very pleasant at home. By the time I got to high school my parents had acquired a lot of debt, and some days I remember mom and dad's fights vividly. I would come home and they would be in the middle of a yelling match. Over what, I was never really sure, but it was taking its toll on me mentally and spiritually. Keep in mind these are the people who in my eyes did no wrong. This conflict continued off and on throughout my high school years. I will never forget the day I came home from school, and there was a repo man outside, with dad on the porch watching as the man drove away in our car. All of this fueled my thoughts to try something to take my mind off of the situation. I started becoming promiscuous, continued to drink and smoke weed, and slowly tried the other drugs I was once afraid of. First was shrooms; then the one I really seemed to enjoy was cocaine. In those days, I never let it get too far out of hand, simply due to athletics. By the grace of God, we all graduated, and then came the biggest question everyone faces around this point: "What am I going to do with the rest of my life?" Looking back at this moment in my life, I had NO idea how to answer this question. I mean, honestly, does anyone?

High school was over, and so was my baseball career. After some elbow problems and my favorite coach's retiring, I decided it was time to give up on that dream. To this day, I miss baseball and the amazing memories I have playing the greatest game there is. Baseball kept me out of a lot of trouble and always gave me something to be passionate about. After graduation we all started to soul search and make moves toward our futures. Well, most of us did. Most everyone went on to college, Roger enlisted in the Marines, and I stuck around Lubbock and started working. I wanted to take a "little" time off from school, but the longer I waited to go back, the less appealing school sounded. Everyone seemed to be making progress and taking steps forward in their lives—everyone but me. I was bouncing around from job to job and drinking a lot, and partying was my main priority. I was losing sight of my faith and just felt like I was floating in mere existence.

The only thing I had going for me at this time was that I was buying the car of my dreams. Before I graduated we moved into some apartments, and a lady who lived in the apartment above us sold me her son's used Ford Probe GT. It was jet black with chrome wheels, and it was fast! This was the only thing that motivated me to keep a job. I take that back—it was this car...and partying. In between jobs, I would go with friends to concerts, stay high for days, and come home jobless. Some months, mom and dad would help with money just so I could afford to make payments.

A little while after I graduated from high school, my dad got transferred to Big Spring, TX. In the midst of my partying, spending all of my money, and having no direction, my parents were leaving. This reality hit me pretty hard. Where was I going to go? What was I going to do now? As always, I knew I had friends to rely on. Heath and Zac were attending Texas Tech University and were there in my time of need. I called them up, explained the situation, and of course they told me to come on over. They were living in a two-bedroom apartment at the time, which meant my bed was the couch. By this time I started working as a stocker at a local grocery store, making just over minimum wage. I agreed to pay Zac and Heath $100 a month, and my car payment was $325 a month. This was a struggle to make ends meet, and let's not forget that I still wanted booze and drugs. Time went by, and I continued to live on their couch. I was spending more money than

I earned on drugs and alcohol, and this led to my missing days at work. I had a pretty cool boss, who was lenient on my behavior. I was scheduled to be at work at 7:00 am, and many days I would show up hung over and sleep in the bathroom. He found me a couple of times and would send me home. Heath would come home from class, and ask, "Did you not have to work today?" Of course I would lie and say, "Nope." Other days I would pretend to go to work, come back when Zac and Heath left, and go back to sleep. Obviously, this lifestyle could not continue. After about six months of staying with my friends, I lost my job. I searched and searched and could find nothing. A month went by, and I missed a car payment. Another month went by, and I missed a car payment and rent. Looking back, I was unintentionally taking advantage of people who cared about me. I didn't even realize it at the time. After two months of my not making a car payment, this sweet lady called and said, "Russell, I need that car back." This was the only thing of value I owned, and I was losing it. Zac and Heath became frustrated with my missing payments and not pulling my weight, so I had to make a move fast. At the time the only choice in my mind was to go stay with mom and dad in Big Spring.

I called mom and told her what was going on. Of course mom said, "Come stay with us for a while, save some money, and get back on your feet." This was not something I wanted to do, but this is a move that would prove to change my life forever.

CHAPTER FOUR

Big Spring, The Demon Speaks

IT WAS IN the spring of 2001 when my parents came to Lubbock to pick me up, and I was off to Big Spring. Walking away from Zac and Heath's apartment, I remember feeling lower than I had in quite a long time. Honestly I felt like a failure. All of my friends seemed to be doing well and making moves closer to their goals. I got in mom and dad's car with all of my belongings, which at the time was a hamper full of clothes, shoes, and pictures. The trip from Lubbock to Big Spring is only about an hour and a half, but it felt like a lifetime. All I could do is think about all the mistakes I had made up to that point and what my next step was going to be. Of course, mom and dad were thrilled to have me staying with them, and they did all they could to help me figure things out.

When my parents moved to Big Spring, they had not found a place to live yet, so the company my dad was working for set them up in a hotel room right next to the station. Here I was, 19 years old, living with my parents in their hotel room. I remember thinking, "Can this get any worse??" The one really positive thing I can tell you about living there was that I became best friends with my parents. I had always known what beautiful people they were, but these were the moments when we really learned about the depth of one another. As in my childhood days, I would see my dad get up at 4 o'clock in the morning to go earn a living for his family. I didn't have a job yet, and he would always tell me, "Don't worry about it. I'll help you get on your feet." Again, my dad has one of the biggest hearts of any man I know. He would leave early in the morning, and mom would get up and cook breakfast on a little single burner electric stovetop. Even on that little grill in that hotel room, my mama made some of the best homemade breakfasts I could possibly imagine. While dad was off working, mom and I spent many hours talking about life and what my plan was. I would always think, "Plan, what plan?" A few weeks went by, and I started getting really stir crazy in that hotel room. I had been looking for work but couldn't find much. Big Spring is not a big town with a lot of opportunities. Go through Big Spring and blink, and you'll miss it. Coming in from Lubbock on highway 87, the first building on the right side is a psychiatric hospital. After that, a few gas stations, then the "drag," a few shopping centers, and then you're out. I searched and searched but was running out of luck. In the meantime to keep myself busy, I started running to the college to use their gym. Between this and smoking weed I always seemed to take my mind off of my current reality.

During my time in Big Spring I would make occasional trips to Lubbock in our old Mercury to see friends and to party. I still had someone in Lubbock to supply me with whatever drugs I needed. I would booze it up with friends, get fixed up with weed and whatever else I needed, and head back to reality. Obviously, my reality wasn't the best situation. I continued to smoke and work out occasionally to pass the time. A few months went by, and mom and dad found a place to live. It was a nice little house in a quiet neighborhood in the middle of Big Spring. It was also around this time dad let me know that his company was hiring. It was a basic grounds and maintenance job and the only opportunity out there, so I jumped on it. Needless to say, it was not my "dream" job, but I had to do something to pull my weight and save money to make a move. When I think about this time in our lives, I recall struggling to the point we couldn't afford our cigarette habit, so we would find half smoked cigarettes and smoke them down to the filter. I know there are people that have it worse, but this was becoming my rock bottom.

By this point in my life I was ready for a big change, and it couldn't come soon enough. I still wasn't interested in school, but I wasn't really sure which direction I wanted to go. One day during a trip back from Lubbock I was listening to a local radio station's commercial about modeling agencies that were going to be auditioning in Dallas. "Make one hundred and fifty thousand dollars a job," the announcer said. I was told a few times growing up, "Hey, you should really consider modeling!" I thought, "What do I have to lose??" For the next couple of weeks we set back as much money as we could to pay for travel and a hotel room. Soon, mom and I were off to Dallas to see if I had what it took to become a model. We showed up at the hotel for the auditions, and during registration they wanted us to have a head shot. I wasn't aware of this, so mom and I went to the gift shop and bought a disposable camera, and she became my photographer. I laugh out loud to myself thinking about mom and me in this hotel room and her telling me, "Okay, pose." We rushed down and had the film developed, and sure enough I had my head shots. We went back to the registration table, and handed over everything they needed to get me started. They told me to be in the lobby at 9 o'clock the next morning, and they would call names alphabetically. They also informed us they hired a DJ and there was a dance that evening. If you know me, you know one of my favorite things in the world to do is dance! Mom and I went and grabbed a bite to eat, and a little beer to loosen me up. I danced the night away with all of the other participants and when it was over shared some laughs with mom over some of the events that night. Just as in my baseball days, mom would always tell me she was so proud of me. Knowing I needed to get some rest, I lay down and tossed and turned until 3 o'clock in the morning.

Feeling like I had only closed my eyes for ten minutes, I heard my alarm buzzing, and it was time to hit the runway. I was so nervous, and everything happened so fast. All I know was they called my name, and I acted as if I had been a model all of my life. I walked back and forth, gave them a smile, and waited to see if I was getting a call back. We each had numbers, and if they called your number, they wanted you to stick around and talk to agents. With fingers crossed, I got a call back from two agencies! My heart raced as I went up to meet them. After meeting with one, they decided it was a no go, but the other one based in Atlanta wanted to move forward! Let's just say, I was ECSTATIC! This was the big break I had been hoping for. The next day we headed back to Big Spring, and I had something new to be passionate about. I started running three to four miles a day and lifting weights when I could get access to the college gym. In the meantime, my agent set me up with a professional photographer in Austin. I touched base with him and figured out the best weekend I could head to Austin and do the shoot. About a month later, mom and I packed up for a road trip to Austin and, as always, left dad behind to work. My parents: no matter what dream I had they always supported it 100 percent and helped me in every way they knew how. I met with the photographer, and he took us to an artsy part of Austin for the photo shoot. To be honest, it was one of the coolest experiences of my life. He had different outfits for me, arranged the most flattering lighting, and guided me to pose this way and that. After a few hours with him, we were done, and he told me I would have the pictures in about two weeks. Sure enough we got them in the mail, and they were awesome, but as soon as I opened them I could see something the modeling agency would have a problem with. After just getting back into working out, but with a few years of munchies and beer drinking, my body wasn't quite where it needed to be.

I sent my agent the pictures, and she called in two days with the response I knew was coming. She told me I needed to drop some weight, so I worked my tail off to get ready for the next shoot. Months went by and I did everything within my power to look the way she said I needed to. The first shoot I did was very expensive, and we didn't have the money for a second, so I asked the agent if it would be okay if the next set of pictures were not professionally done. She said that was fine, so once again my mom became my photographer.

We went to a park with some old train tracks where there was a bit more "scenery." I felt I was ready, and this was my shot at becoming a model and moving forward with my life. We snapped the pictures, sent them off, and a week later I got a call. It was the agent telling me, "From the look of things, we've decided we are not moving forward with the process." My heart sank into my stomach, and I hit a wall headfirst. After this call I lost all motivation to move forward in my life. All I could think about was all the loss and negativity in my life. Throughout my life we had been through so much as a family, and now in my early adulthood it was happening to me. As in my childhood, things would seem so wonderful, so beautiful, and then a wrench would be thrown into the spokes. There would be days life couldn't seem to get any better, and then we would lose it all. I would just pray, "Why God, why does there seem to be this black cloud over me and my family? We always thank You for what we have, and we don't have much. What lesson are You trying to teach me?" This is when things really took a turn for the worse in my life.

With no goals and nothing to bring me joy, I continued down the road of drugs and alcohol because that was the only thing that seemed to numb what I was going through. I hid the drugs quite well from mom and dad, and I would even put liquor under my mattress to drink when they went to bed. I quit my job and would come up with whatever reason I could to take a trip to Lubbock. I would return to Lubbock, and friends would ask, "Are you okay?" They would also say things like, "You don't seem like yourself." I would always tell them I was fine and go back to partying to forget everything. Even after I let Heath and Zac down, I remember that Heath always asked about my life, trying to give me spiritual encouragement. I always appreciated his efforts, but I was running as far away from God as I could. He had not come to help me yet, and I was blaming Him for everything. All the while, I could hear His voice. It was faint, but it was always there. I continued to run, and run as far away as I could by drinking myself into oblivion, falling into sex and drugs—anything to wash Him out. Yet He was always there. I now know that whatever you focus on will only expand. All I could seem to focus on was how God deserted my family and me, so I was going to show Him I didn't need Him. I can't even truly recall how long this lifestyle continued, but it all came to a head on Thanksgiving Day in 2002.

I got up that day looking forward to watching football with dad, smoking a little weed, and then eating what was sure to be an amazing Thanksgiving meal. The house was filled with the smell of turkey, ham, dressing, corn bread, dinner rolls, green bean casserole, and of course mom's homemade apple pie. Dad was on the couch, and as I walked in he said, "Hey, bub, how ya feeling today?" Since it was Thanksgiving I was actually feeling pretty good that day. I went into the kitchen where mom was hard at work and gave her a hug, told her I loved her, and how I couldn't wait for dinner. I grabbed some iced tea and went back into the living room with dad. We watched the pregame and simply enjoyed his being off for the day. I finished my tea and was eager to go get some weed before we ate. I told dad, "Hey, I'll be back in a bit." Dad said, "Okay, bub, we'll be here." He smiled as I walked out the door, and within just a couple of hours, my whole world was turned upside down.

I was on a mission to go get some weed and smoke before we ate dinner. A girl I knew who lived across the street told me she knew a guy who could get us some really good stuff. I got into her car, and we were on our way to pick it up. We arrived at the dealer's house, and suddenly I heard that little voice telling me not to go in there. I ignored it like I had for so long, and this is when the battle for my soul began. I walked into the house expecting to get a bag of weed and go home. The dealer was uneasy about my being there as much as

I was about being there. He asked, "Who are you?" with a hateful tone and sinister look in his eye. My "friend" explained that I just came with her to buy a little weed. He told me, "No one comes into my house and buys anything without smoking with me first." I obliged and he proceeded to light a joint. As we smoked, the awkward tension continued, and finally we finished the joint. I got my stuff and we were out. The moment we got into her car, I began to feel different. Not the way I normally felt on pot. I felt fearful, disoriented, and confused to the point I looked in the mirror to see if "I" was still sitting there. When I looked into the mirror, it was not my own reflection I saw looking back at me. My thoughts began to race, "What was happening to me? Why is this happening to me?" In that very moment I felt as if something beyond my control had taken over my thoughts.

I couldn't look at the girl I was with, I didn't want to look at myself in the mirror, and I told her get me home as fast as possible. She dropped me off, and I stood outside my parents' house for a few minutes trying to pull myself together. As I walked by their car I caught my reflection in the car window, and it terrified me. I rushed inside where dad was still sitting on the couch, and mom was still in the kitchen. I went straight to my bedroom and closed the door. I lay on my bed and heard a voice saying, "Hurt yourself, hurt yourself, hurt yourself." I started to cry, and the voice got louder. This time it said, "KILL yourself!" My dad knocked on my door, and asked, "Bub, everything okay?" I said, "Yes, dad, everything is fine." Everything was not fine. There was a spiritual war happening in my soul, and I didn't know what to do. I dried my eyes, and hoping that seeing mom and dad would help, I went into the kitchen where they were. The first thing that caught my eye was the carving knife, and I heard the voice again. "KILL yourself!" I told mom and dad I didn't feel well, and went back to my room. I remember their coming into my room periodically and asking if there was anything they could do to help. The answer was always, no. This was something way bigger than anyone could help me with. This was the moment I found out how strong my God is.

The voices continued, and the only

thing I knew to do was to pray, to pick up my Bible and read. I opened my Bible with no specific scripture in mind, and the first verse I read was Matthew 5:3: "Blessed are the poor in spirit, for theirs is the kingdom of heaven." I continued to read verses 3-10, and these words started to flood my soul. I also started watching a "Gaither" video my parents had in the living room. As I lay on my bed and prayed, the video started playing, "Oh victory in Jesus, my savior forever, He sought me and bought me, with His redeeming love." There was so much power in those words! I sang these words over and over and over.

Singing this song provided the only time there was even a little peace in my soul. I recall hating going to sleep because I would have the most vivid, evil dreams I had ever had in my life. My dreams would show me doing what the voices were telling me to do--hurting my parents, the people I cherished the most in my life. The nightmares of my hurting myself were the most vivid. I would wake up in a cold sweat and pray, "God, please protect me. Protect my heart, protect my mind, protect my spirit. Help me fight this

battle, because I can NOT do it alone."
The struggle continued, and the inner
battle was more than I can even put into
words. It seemed the more I prayed and
read my Bible, the more my demon would
try to tear me down. Mom suggested that
I see a psychiatrist, and at this point I
wanted help. It helped a little just to sit
down and talk about some of what I was
going through. For some reason, though, I
never wanted to tell him about the voices I
heard. I was fearful that I might be sent to a
psychiatric hospital, away from my parents.
I met with the doctor a few times, and he
decided to put me on medication. All it
seemed to do was make me want to sleep,
and sleeping was sometimes the last thing
I wanted to do because of the nightmares.
After a few visits, I stopped seeing him and
stopped taking the medication since I felt
it wasn't helping. Now I'm not saying that
all people should stop taking medication,
but for me it didn't seem to be doing what
I'd hoped it would, and that was to stop the
voices. These thoughts were a perpetual
cycle, and I had to do something to try to
end it.

It was then that I told God, "I give this

battle over to You 100 percent! I am yours, and if You save my life, I will do everything I can to show You my love for You!" That is exactly what He did. He literally saved my life! As the weeks went by, I would pray this prayer a few times a day. I also began to talk to mom and dad about ALL that was going on with me. When I began to have suicidal thoughts, I would immediately get up and go for a run. I had to do something to break these thoughts. Slowly, day-by-day, the "bad" voices seemed to become quieter, and "His" voice became clearer. I started to develop a routine. I would wake up every day at 7:00 am, read my Bible, pray and meditate, and thank God for all of the blessings in my life. After that I would feel more self worth than I had ever felt in my life! I was ready to take on the day. I became obsessed with running and lifting weights. I did everything I could to keep my mind focused on all the beauty in this life, so I would run a trail in Big Spring that led to the top of a hill. There at the top of this hill were some of the best one-on-one times I had ever spent with God, and He spoke to my soul. I started to feel an overwhelming sense of peace in my life.

As I was starting to feel alive again, I remember dad going and hitting golf balls in a field by the house. After one of my morning runs, I asked dad if he wouldn't mind taking me with him to hit balls. He said, "SURE, let's go!" Even during my baseball days, dad always wanted to teach me how to play golf, but I never had an interest back then. We arrived at the field with a pitching wedge, a seven iron, and a driver. Dad put the pitching wedge in my hand, showed me the proper grip and stance, and I swung away. That day we spent a few hours in that field, hitting hundreds of golf balls. Golf came pretty naturally to me after coming from a baseball background. To say the least, I was hooked! On the days dad had to work, I would go out to that field and hit balls for hours, and just thank God for all the beauty I had in this life, thanking Him especially for that very moment. Once I became pretty consistent at just striking the ball, dad decided it was time to take me out to actually play. Even if I played horribly, these are times with my dad I will never forget. There would be days on the course I would get so frustrated, but then I would stop and look around, in awe of the beauty around me. The green trees blowing in the wind, the birds singing, even just the blue sky. These were all sights I had taken for granted, but never again! As dad continued to teach me the game of golf, and I continued to improve, I realized this was my new passion. It gave me something I hadn't had since I quit baseball, and that was a goal. My new goal was to play pro/semi-professional golf. I worked hard at it day in and day out, and all the while I could hear my God saying, "It's time for your next chapter in life, Russell." One day as I prayed on top of that hill, His voice became so clear and said, "It's time for you to move back to Lubbock." I went home and that entire day I prayed for a way this could happen. I had no money and no transportation. That night around 11:00 pm, I went into the living room and told mom and dad, "It's time for me to go." They knew it was time. I called one of my best friends, Lance, and asked if I could stay with him for a while. He was excited to hear from me and said, "Come on, bro, my door will be open." In the living room of the house I went through Hell in, mom, dad, and I said a prayer for my journey. We shed many tears, and I remember hugging them like I would never see them again. After the prayer, dad handed me the keys to that old Mercury, and that night I hit the road with a purpose.

CHAPTER FIVE

New Beginnings

DURING THAT DRIVE back to Lubbock, I had never been this excited to take on a challenge. My goal was to get a job at a golf course so I could afford to play as much as I needed to, and chase my dream of being a pro golfer. I arrived at Lance's one bedroom efficiency just after midnight. He greeted me at the door with a hug and a cold beer. Lance had always been one of my best friends, and this is when we got to know each other on an even deeper level. That night I explained to him what all had happened to me, and it felt so good to talk about it and share my testimony. We sat up and almost talked all night, as I told him what my plan was. I went to bed around 3 o'clock in the morning and could not wait for 7:00 in the morning to come so I could start the next chapter of my life. I maintained my routine of waking up at 7:00 am, reading my Bible and being grateful for God's bringing me to this point in my life. Immediately after I had my quiet time, I began the search for a new job and a new beginning. I went to just about every golf course in Lubbock, TX, but all were fully staffed. I began to get a little down and started to doubt myself. Finally I came to the last course on the list, and said this prayer, "God, You brought me out of Hell and brought me to this point. I trust You." I took a deep breath, opened the door to the pro shop, and there behind the counter was the dad of one of my old childhood friends. I walked in, and he said, "Hi, I'm Jay, can I help you?" I said, "Yes sir! My name is Russell Butler, and I would love to work for you." It was then he realized who I was, shook my hand, and even pulled me in for a hug. We laughed as we reminisced about the good times we had on our street. Turns out he was the head pro of the course and was delighted to give me a job. I walked out of that shop and looked into the sky and just said, "Thank You." I went home super excited to tell Lance I had found a job and would start first thing in the morning.

It's amazing what happens when you trust in where God is leading you and

just put one foot in front of the other. I
started the next day as Jay's new cart boy.
I would pick up range balls, wash the golf
carts, help clean the pro shop, and any
other duties Jay called me to do. I LOVED
every minute of it! On the days I worked
I would either go in early and get off in
the afternoon, or go in that evening and
work until we closed at midnight. This is
the only course in Lubbock with a lighted
par three back nine. Either way, whichever
shift I worked I would either show up early
and practice or stay after and play nine
holes. I would call dad, and he would be so
jealous because I was getting to play all the
time for free! I called mom and dad often
to let them know life was amazing. This
was one of the happiest times in my life.
I worked for Jay as a cart boy for almost
a year before a spot opened up in the pro
shop. Once this position became available,
I was delighted to take it on headfirst. The
longer I was in the golf business, the more
I learned the business and felt the urge to
do more. I was still pursuing the dream
of going pro, but in the meantime I loved
helping others develop their swings and
learn to play the game. This inspired me to

take my PAT (player ability test), the first step in a long process to becoming a PGA professional. I loved teaching and helping others so much, especially kids, that I was willing to do whatever it took to earn this title. The player ability test involves playing two rounds at a certain course, and your score must be lower than the target score set for the course. If you've ever played regular golf and tournament golf, you know they are two different things. I would take this test three times over the course of two years before I passed. This is when I started to realize that I was only a decent player under pressure, and you have to be more than decent to hang with the big boys. This is when I really developed a love for teaching the game, which brought to light my love for helping others. Over the next couple of years, as I was getting goals dialed in and loving what I was doing and where I was going, I was also catching up on time missed with my best friends.

Lance and I continued to live together in our one-bedroom efficiency, and Heath, Zac, and Big Mike lived in a house where we all congregated. Along with these guys, Skyler, Michael Salazar (Sal), and Alan were all still in Lubbock as well. We got together often at Zac and Heath's for a game of pool and some beer pong. It was like old times, but I was in a much better place. These were some great times as we all were making moves in the right direction for our futures. We stayed up until almost dawn sometimes talking about life and how amazing it was. All of us dated off and on, and I can still remember when things didn't seem to work out with a girl we all turned to Heath for advice. He was never too busy and always willing to listen. All of us were this way with one another, but Heath just had a way of making things make sense. As we moved forward in life, we kept our noses to the grindstone and held each other to the highest of standards. If one of us slipped we could always count on one another to pick each other up. This is true friendship, and I was/am blessed to have such friends.

A couple of years went by and we continued to make progress to become the men we knew we were called to be. One night after a late shift at the golf course I came home, and Lance seemed kind of quiet. I walked in, set my stuff down, and he said, "Hey, bro, I want to talk to you about something." I said, "Of course, what's going on?" He pulled out a piece of paper and got a little choked up, and said, "I want you to be the first to know, I have enlisted in the Marines, and I will be deployed after boot camp." A few years after 9/11 Lance said he was ready to fight. I stood there silent for a bit thinking about my best friend's going to war. I was proud and scared at the same time. I knew his mind was made up, so all I could do was give him a hug and tell him, "I support you 100 percent!" We hugged and shed some tears—and put away quite a few beers if my memory serves me well. Lance's brother Micah, another one of my brothers, always laughed at Lance and me as we would sit in our little apartment and listen to music and drink wine *like a couple of women*. I remember it was a very hard day for all of us when Lance left for boot camp. Lance, like Heath, is another one of our friends who is the glue for our relationships. Our brother Roger had been in the Marines since we graduated from high school, and now we were sending Lance off and praying for his protection.

I stayed in the apartment for one month after Lance left. While I was finishing out my lease, Alan called me and said I could come live with him and his brother Carlos. To say the least, I was elated to hear this news. As you may recall, I met Alan in seventh grade, and we hit it off immediately. Growing up with Alan, his family became my second family. Well, I guess you could say I had a few families, because all of my friends' families accepted me and loved me like one of their own. So I was blessed to be staying with Alan and "Los." While living there we would enjoy many nights in the backyard with friends playing the guitar and singing the night away. Every day I would still wake up at 6 or 7:00 am and thank God for bringing me to this point in my life. While living here I continued my education in the golf business. I worked lots of hours and made pretty good money. I was dating off and on and simply enjoying life. I would bring a girl to meet my friends, and that was the test. Usually they knew as well as I did if it was going to last.

Some years went by and life continued this way. Wake up, be thankful, and make moves closer to my goals. I would often receive letters and phone calls from Lance telling me about his life and what he was dealing with. One of the most terrifying calls I received from him was his telling me he was being deployed to Ramadi, Iraq. At this point in the war, Ramadi had become the most dangerous place to be in Iraq. That call sent chills down my spine, but I told him I loved him and would see him when he returned.

Over the course of the next few years my faith was always being tested. As I mentioned earlier, my dreams of becoming a PGA professional were put on hold year after year because I was unable to pass the PAT. I began to worry and doubt if I was even on the right track. Then one day on my way to work, I was driving along when all of the sudden my engine caught on fire in my little Ford Mercury. I started to revert to my old way of thinking and become the victim. I was thinking God was punishing me for something. I remember even at one point while my car was on fire asking God, "Why are You allowing this to happen to me? I've been so faithful." I called into work that day and made a call to Alan to come pick me up. On the ride to the house Alan let me know that his dad fixed up used cars and sold them. The very next day mom and dad came in for a visit, and took me out to lunch. After lunch we headed out to Alan's dad's house to see if he had anything I could afford. Sure enough he had a 1999 Ford Explorer Sport, and it was in great condition! We all hopped in and took it for a test drive, and when we got back to his house he told me how much he wanted as a down payment. I remember that it was about all the money I had, but I was more than grateful to be buying my own car. When I got home, in my OWN car, I sat back in the seat and felt an overwhelming feeling of gratefulness. I had a home, I had a job, I had a car. The one thing I felt I was still searching for was the love of my life.

It was spring of 2004 when we received word that Lance was coming home from the war! I got a call from him late one night, and he told me, "I can't wait to see all my brothers and catch up over a beer." All of us guys got together and decided it needed to be the best welcome home party ever! When he returned, we were all so anxious to see him. He called and told me his folks were going to pick him up from the airport, and they were having dinner, but as soon as they were finished he wanted to see his brothers and go out. All of us were in Lubbock on the day he arrived and were ready to celebrate. I picked Lance up from his house around 8:30, and we started up right where we left off. I can't put into words how grateful I was that my friend was home. We chatted on the way to Heath's house, and when we arrived ALL the boys were out front holding beers and ready to see our brother. As the song goes, "The boys are back in town!" We caught up over some games of pool; Heath proceeded to dominate everyone. Yes, he was even amazing at pool. After a few games we asked Lance where he wanted to go, and he decided on a place with the best margaritas in town. Off we were to continue the celebration of our old friend returning home. The hours went by, margarita after margarita, beer after beer, shot after shot, and now it was time to dance! When all of my friends and I get together, dancing is what we do best. We packed in the car and headed downtown where there was supposed to be the best DJ in Lubbock and good drink specials. The place was packed, but we made a spot on the dance floor like we always do. There we were, all twelve of us having the time of our lives. We danced for hours, continued to have drinks, and then things took a turn for the worse. As I was dancing, apparently there was a girl who said something about my being cute and a good dancer. I guess her boyfriend heard this and wasn't happy. He said something directed toward me, but I didn't hear it. The last person who should have heard it did: Lance. Lance was fresh out of war and slightly on edge. When he heard what the boyfriend said, he confronted him about it. I was completely unaware of this situation, as was everyone else. The club was about to close, and half of our friends decided to go out of the back entrance because there was a food truck near that exit. So they went one way, and Lance, Sal, Micah, Heath, our friend Melissa, and I all went out the front. As we are about to get in the car, Micah and I heard Lance having words with the guy from inside the club. I went to intervene and explain to him that this was not the best night because Lance had just returned from Iraq and we had had a lot to drink, as I'm sure he did as well. By the time I got involved, I realized this guy had recruited quite a few of his friends to deal with the five of us. As I'm trying to calm the situation down, two guys came up behind Lance, ready to take him down, and I knew there was no other option than to defend my brother. As they rushed him, I swung as hard as I could to stop the guy on the left. Next thing I knew I was at the bottom of a dog pile, and these guys were using my head as a soccer ball. Every time I tried to get up, I would feel another foot to the back of my head and my forehead bounced off of the pavement. I could feel the gravel digging into my head, and at this point I started to worry for my life. To this day, I have a pretty jagged scar to remind me how blessed I am to be alive. As the brawl went on with me at the bottom of the pile, we were outnumbered by quite a bit. It was then our friend Melissa realized if someone didn't get me out of this situation it could possibly end worse than it did. So as she recalls, she jumped on top of the pile and bit whomever she could to get to me. In the meantime, Lance, Micah, and

Sal were swinging for the fences.

When I emerged from the bottom of the pile, thanks to Melissa, all I remember was seeing Lance holding a guy in an arm bar, as two of his friends punched him in the back of the head. I heard Lance say, "If your friends don't stop punching me, I will break your arm!" Sure enough they did not stop, and I saw Lance use some of his training full force. I stumbled around for a bit before I realized how bad I was bleeding. I looked at Melissa and said, "I need to get to the hospital as soon as possible!" She rushed me to her car, and the last thing I saw was Sal throwing punches wildly to protect himself from two guys.

Once we got in the car I thought I would be okay to go home and simply wash the wound, so I told Melissa "Just drive me home." We arrived at the house, and the guys were soon to follow. When they walked in I was in the bathroom examining the damage done to my forehead. As soon as I looked, I knew I was in need of medical attention. Lance rushed in behind me, and all I remember at this point was his screaming and rushing to the backyard, punching the fence because he felt he had let me down. It was pure chaos. I asked Melissa to please drive me to the ER. When we arrived, I was holding a towel covered in blood, so they got Sal and me in right away. I waited and waited for the doctor; when he walked in he told me, "It's so bad, there is not enough skin to stitch up." He cleaned the wound, dressed it, and then sent me on my way. The next day we planned on everyone meeting at Heath's to have lunch. Those of us who were in the brawl of the century walked in battered and bruised. I had a bandaged forehead and two black eyes from the swelling. Lance, I recall, had a black eye with a gigantic knot on his forehead. I'm sure we all looked as if we had been hit by a freight train. We all talked about the fight, and how lucky we were nothing worse happened. To this day I thank God for surrounding me with His angel army. Thinking back on it, He had His angels watching over all of us that night. If you think about me at the bottom of that pile, full of adrenaline mixed with alcohol, the situation could have turned out much worse than it did.

A week went by, and we were healing up nicely. We decided it was time to throw

Lance an "official" welcome-home party.
Now I don't remember a lot of details about
this party other than the fact that I met the
future Mrs. Butler. While we were busy
playing pool, dancing, and having a blast,
Big Mike told me his girlfriend was coming
over with her friend Monica. I didn't think
much of it at the time, but an hour went
by, and in walked this girl. I was in the
backyard at the time but made a quick
entry back into the living room. I tried to
act nonchalantly about the situation, but
I knew I had to introduce myself to her. I
danced my way up, stuck out my hand to
this quiet girl, and said, " Hi, I'm Russell,
and I'm glad you're here." Despite the
bandage on my forehead and two black
eyes, she said, "I'm Monica, it's nice to
meet you." Then just as quickly as I had
come in, I went back outside to catch my
breath. We made eye contact off and on
through the night, and finally she came
outside and sat next to me on the swing in
Heath's back yard. There we discovered
that this wasn't just a coincidence, but we
were destined to meet that night. We sat on
that swing while the world turned around
us. Time seemed to stand still as we talked

about EVERYTHING. We discovered my dad worked with her grandparents on the railroad, her mom was the secretary at my elementary school, and growing up we were only one social group away from one another. I had not felt a connection with a girl like this in my life. There was no awkward silence, no false pretenses. We were just in the moment. What a beautiful moment it was. We swung back and forth until four in the morning, talking about everything from religion to what we wanted our firstborn child's name to be. This beautiful woman who captivated every part of my soul would soon become my wife.

CHAPTER SIX

Love and Loss

AFTER THE NIGHT was over, Monica and I decided we had to get together as soon as possible. We exchanged numbers, and I told the boys I had just met the girl of my dreams. Remember my saying that meeting my friends was always the test? Well, they all met Monica that night, and there was no question about it: she was a keeper! The next night there was a really good band playing at a local pub, so we decided that was the plan for the night. I wanted to call Monica so badly but didn't want to seem too eager. That being said, I just told Big Mike to make sure his lady came, and to make sure Monica came with her. We got to the bar, and all I could think about was this girl named Monica. I kept bugging Mike, are they coming? Are they coming? Then while I was out on the dance floor, I peeked over the crowd and saw her walking in. My heart pounded in

my chest like I had never met her, and I
was nervous all over again. I swallowed
the big lump in my throat and approached
her again. This time I had a beer for her,
and I asked her if she would like to dance.
She quietly responded, "Of course," and
we danced together as if we had danced
together all of our lives. Things just seemed
too perfect about this girl. I kept trying to
find flaws, but they simply were not there.
The night slipped away while we danced,
song after song. The conversation picked
right back up from the night before, and we
never skipped a beat. The bar was about to
close, and as everyone was getting ready
to head back to Heath's house, Monica
asked me, " Would you like to come meet
my mom?" I was absolutely terrified, but
I said, "Of course." Little did I know that
the night before the party, Monica told her
mom, "I'm going to meet the man of my
dreams tonight." Now I was on my way to
meet her mom at 2:30 in the morning with
a bandage on my head and two black eyes.
I met Monica at her mom's doorstep with
my stomach in knots. The door opened,
and I heard the sweetest, "Well, y'all come
on in now!" with the strongest West Texas

accent I had ever heard. Her mom offered us a beer while we sat and told her about the night. Of course her mom was firing questions at me left and right, but all the while being super kind to me. We all got a big laugh out of the fact that our families' paths had crossed several times but never made the connection. I remember loving her mom instantly. Not long after my meeting her folks, it was time for her to meet mine. It was about a year after I moved back from Big Spring that mom and dad were soon to follow. Mom wanted to be close to her family, so dad put in a transfer to come back to Lubbock. They found a place in no time, and it was a blessing to have them so close again, especially after meeting the love of my life. The day we were on our way to meet them for lunch, Monica was afraid they wouldn't like her, and they were afraid she wouldn't like them. Of course they chatted like they had known one another for years. Mom made her typical feast with some iced tea, and for that moment all the world was right. A few weeks later it was time for me to meet the rest of her family, her big brother Mike and sister Melaney. We were at the same pub where we had our first dance, and as we sat at the bar Monica said, "They're here." I looked back from my seat, and the first people I saw walk in were her sister's boyfriend Shawn and a family friend, Jabbo. To say the least both of these men were more than intimidating. After these two walked in then came her sister, then her brother. I hit it off with all of the guys almost immediately, but her sister seemed pretty reluctant to give me a chance. I sat down with them, and after a couple of beers her sister told me, "If you ever hurt my sister, I will castrate you." Not in those exact words. As the night went on her sister let down her guard, and I knew she said what she did because they are the best of friends.

Over the next few weeks Monica and I were together every opportunity we had, and every time I saw her I was as giddy as if it were the first time we met. Weeks turned into months, and after only four short months I knew I wanted her to be my wife. I'll never forget going to her dad's house knowing I was going to ask for her hand in marriage. My father-in-law is one of the greatest men I've ever known. That was, by far, the most nervous I had been in my entire life. Let me give you a quick rundown of my now father-in-law. George Michael Barecky, Jr., is a Vietnam veteran, super intelligent, quiet, a hell of a cook, and most of all protects and cares for his family like a real father does. Needless to say, after I had dated Monica for only four short months he still wasn't sure about me. The day I was going to ask for her hand, I walked into his house and my knees quivered. My palms were sweaty, and every time I passed him in his recliner, I wanted to throw up. The rest of her family--mom, brother, and sister--were all there and knew that's what I was there to do. They would all get a big laugh out of my pacing back and forth in the hallway, waiting for my opportunity. Finally I saw George get up from his recliner and go to the kitchen, and I knew it was now or never. I walked into the kitchen, and my voice trembled as I said, "George, I love your daughter with all of my heart and would do anything in this world for her. I am asking you, her daddy, for her hand in marriage." He looked down at the floor and looked back at me with watery eyes, and said, "She is my baby girl, and I trust that you will take care of her. If you break that trust...well, just don't break that trust." I took the deepest breath I think I've ever taken in my life, and we hugged in his kitchen. After that he said to me in Czech, "Date si pivo?" which means, "Would you like a beer?" We all gathered in the kitchen and said cheers to new beginnings.

It was Thanksgiving in 2005 when I asked her to be my bride. It's pretty ironic that Thanksgiving reminds me of one of the best and worst days of my life. It was at her memaw's house that her whole family gathered to celebrate this day. Her family is one of the closest families I know, and something they do every Thanksgiving is to circle in the living room and to tell one thing they are thankful for. All family members relate how thankful they are for so much in their lives. It was my turn, and the emotions were overwhelming. I thought back to that Thanksgiving Day in Big Spring and how far God brought me. He brought me to this point in my life where I was surrounded by people who loved me; most of all, he brought me to the love of my life. There I stood in that living room trying to control the tears and emotions.

I told everyone how thankful I was for that very moment, and in that moment I took Monica's hand, got on one knee and said, " Monica, I love you more than I can put into words. I thank God each day for another breath of life and for allowing me to find you. You are all I want in this life, and you would make me the happiest man in the world if you would be my wife." That Thanksgiving Day she said yes, and a new chapter in our lives began.

We dated for four short months, and were engaged for one year. On September 22, 2006, Monica and I became one flesh in the sight of God and all of our loved ones. Our wedding was one to remember. All of the love was felt that beautiful September day as we said our, *"I do's."* After an emotion-filled ceremony, we walked into the reception hall to find out that my boys had hired a mariachi band, and they played as we entered the room. Immediately I knew this would be a party for the ages. Over 100 people danced the night away to mariachi classics, and a DJ followed. A few days later we were off to Jamaica to celebrate our new beginning.

After the honeymoon was over, our

relationship was instantly put to the test. When we returned to Lubbock I was offered a second assistant pro job at a more upscale course in Lubbock. The starting pay was less than I had hoped for, but I figured after a year or so, I would work my way up and there would be more opportunity. After that year went by, I started realizing this might not have been the best decision for us at the time. My pay had not increased much, but our bills had. It was our first year of marriage and we were already living paycheck to paycheck and digging ourselves into a hole. A few more months went by, and we had a decision to make: stay in the house we were in, or move in with my father-in-law to put back some money. We decided we had no other choice than to move in with my father-in-law. I began to think, "Am I doomed to live this life struggling daily to make ends meet?" This added stress caused me to stress eat and both of us to drink a little more than we should. I was putting on weight like crazy and felt like a shell of the man I knew I was. This led to our first few arguments as a married couple, and it was then I started tuning out and blaming God again for everything going wrong. I knew I had to find a different stress relief and start finding a way to dig us out of this hole. Some of my friends started doing this new fitness program called CrossFit that not only pushed a person physically but more so mentally. The more I learned about it, and the more I got involved, I started figuring out this was how I wanted to help people. Within my first year of doing this program I lost 40 pounds and began to feel alive again! I started realizing it was not just changing me physically, but emotionally—and most of all spiritually. This also brought me to the realization that this is one way I was called to help others change their lives! After a little over a year working at that last golf course, I started making an exit strategy to enter the personal training world.

I quit the job at the previous course to take on a specific teaching job at a local golf club shop. Things were okay there, but I still felt a calling to help people on a deeper level. As a few months went by, I showed up to work unenthused and would count down the minutes until I would get off and could go work out. The longer I was at this job, the more I could feel God pulling me in the direction of fitness, and helping others achieve their own life goals. I knew my boss could tell I wasn't happy in the position, and he tried everything he could to motivate me. Six months into this job, I stalled out. My sales were going down dramatically, I lost quite a few clients, and my boss was more than unsatisfied with my performance.

It was October 29, 2008, that events in my life came crashing in again. Let me tell you why this day will stand out as one of the worst days of my life. I came into work that morning and could tell my boss was avoiding me. He was back in office for a couple of hours, and had not said one word to me. After I finished with my second client that morning, my boss finally came to me and said, " I would like to speak to you before you go to lunch today." I said, "Okay" and went to meet my last client for that morning. I taught the lesson, and tried to be as helpful and as attentive as I could, but I did not have in me. The lesson was over, and it was time for me to meet my boss in his office. I had a pretty good feeling about what was coming. I sat down, and he laid it on the line, " Russell, as you know, your numbers have dropped significantly. I don't feel you are benefiting this company anymore, and I would like you to finish out today as your last day with us." My mind started racing, and my heart was heavy. I had to go home and tell my wife and father-in-law that I was going to be without a job. The question started coming to my mind again, "Where are You, God?" I went for a short lunch and came back early to call my afternoon clients to see if they could come in early. I was ready for this last day to be done, so I could figure out the next step for my wife and me.

I finished my last day and drove home dreading having to tell Monica and my father-in-law this news. Instead of taking a step forward, I felt we were taking steps backward. I came in with my head down and feeling like a failure. Monica greeted me at the door, and asked, "What's wrong, baby?" Letting out a big sigh and swallowing my pride, I told her the news. She didn't look down on me or get upset. Like the amazing woman she is, she told me, "It will be okay. God will provide, and we will make it through this." I cried

as I told her I was sorry, and I wanted
to give her more. We held each other in
our bedroom and began to pray. George
would be home soon, and I was mustering
up the courage to tell him the situation I
had gotten us into. He came in tired from
work, and the last thing I wanted to do
was tell him I lost my job. This man was
kind enough to let his daughter, and now
son-in-law, live in his house, and now here
I was without a job. I saw him sit down in
his recliner ready to relax, and I know I
had to tell him right then. Walking into the
living room I was getting choked up, but I
managed to get out, " George, can I talk to
you a minute?" He said, "Sure, what's up?"
My heart sank to the pit of my stomach as
the words came out, " I lost my job today."
He sat there quiet for a bit, and reassured
me, "My home is your home, but you need
to have a job as soon as possible." Like the
awesome man he is, he stood up and gave
me a hug, and told me it would be okay.
Full of shame, I went back to the room
and lay down on the bed, so uncertain of
my future. It seemed like I only closed my
eyes for just a bit, when Monica walked in
with the most earth shattering news I could

possibly receive.

She woke me up from my nap and said, "Baby, I have something to tell you." The tears streamed down her face as she said, "My mom just called. She just found out that Heath shot himself." On October 29, 2008, I lost my dear friend Robert Heath Stewart to suicide. As I type these words, seven years later, all of the emotions I felt that day come rushing back. This had been one of the hardest days of my life, and now if I had any good emotions left they were ripped from my soul. Words cannot express the grief I felt on that day. All I wanted to do was to call my friend and have him answer his phone, but it was not going to happen. I began to cry out to God, "WHY, WHY, WHY?" The sun was setting when Robert, Heath's dad, called us men to come over to try to explain the events of that horrible day. It was a day I will never forget. I will let Robert share the details leading up to that dark day.

CHAPTER SEVEN

Robert Heath Stewart

WE ALL CAME to see Heath's family, and Robert wanted his best friends (brothers) to know what happened. When we arrived, all of his family was standing outside, holding one another in prayer. All I remember thinking was, "Is this real?" I just kept waiting for Heath to come out and hug me, but he wasn't going to. It started to hit me that my brother, the one I always counted on in hard times...I was never going to see him again. I was never going to hear his voice again or see his beautiful smile. I was never going to share dreams, laughs, and tears with him ever again. None of this made sense. "Not Heath." Not the pillar of strength we all knew. I remember getting out of the car and hugging Robert, asking "Is he really gone?" We wept together. All of us men sat down on the curb while Robert tried to gather himself and tried to put into words

what happened. He told us that Heath
had not been out of the house much in a
few days and just didn't seem like himself.
Apparently this had been going on for a
couple of months, but Heath had not told
anyone about what was happening to him.
Not his family, not us brothers, no one.
Robert said he had become more and more
secluded and shut off to the world with
nothing much to say. This automatically
did not sound like the Heath we all knew-
-the vibrant, loving, laughing, smiling,
caring person we all knew Heath to be.

Robert told us that it all started around
the end of August. Heath had a good job
working at a bank. One day he called
Robert almost in a panic telling him, "I
need you to get me out of this job today!"
This wasn't like Heath at all. Heath was
always a man who handled situations
with courage and pride and with respect
for everyone involved. Wanting Robert
to handle the situation for him seemed a
little strange. Robert tried to reason with
him and ask what was going on. Heath
was adamant about Robert's getting him
out of the job that day. Finally Robert told
him, "Okay, son, I will email your boss

requesting you be let go." He told us that from that day forward he watched Heath go into a fast downhill spiral. The Heath I always knew was very well dressed and always took care of his appearance. Robert told us that within two weeks of his quitting the job, Heath's appearance changed dramatically. His face became sunken, he lost quite a bit of weight, and his overall demeanor was drab. As Robert was explaining this, it began to sound all too familiar. I recalled when my depression/ voices started, I cared nothing about the outside world, and this affected my appearance. The last thing I was concerned about was how I looked. All I could think of at that time were the voices and dreadful nightmares. As the days went on, Robert said, he knew something was wrong, but he just expected Heath to snap out of it. But he didn't. Robert tried to get Heath to do little tasks around the house and take him to work with him occasionally just to keep his mind occupied. One day while Robert, his brother, and Heath were working in a field about an hour from Lubbock, something odd happened. Robert's brother called out to him, while pointing at Heath who was a few yards away chopping at weeds with a hoe. He was yelling at Heath, "Rattlesnake!" Robert tried to draw Heath's attention to the snake only a few feet from him. Robert said that Heath seemed as if he were in another world as he slowly lifted his head and calmly watched the snake slither by him. Robert's brother told Robert, "I'm not sure what's going on with Heath, but you need to get him out of here. If a pump jack comes on and he's in that mental state, not watching, he could be killed." Robert agreed and loaded Heath into the truck to head back to Lubbock. As they were driving back, Robert was pondering what had just happened, but Heath hadn't said one word. Robert told us he looked over at Heath and said, "Heath, can you give me one word, just one word, that sums up how you're feeling?" He said Heath's cheeks sank in as he started to rub his chest. Twenty minutes went by, and he still hadn't answered the question. Finally, thirty minutes later, Heath said, "Lost." Robert said to Heath, "What do you mean, lost?" They continued on the drive, and Heath began to rub his chest again and didn't answer the question. Then another thirty minutes went by, and as they were pulling into Lubbock, Heath said, "Spiritually."

Robert couldn't believe what Heath had just said. All of us who knew Heath well knew him as a prayer warrior and a very strong Christian. Robert told Heath, "Son, you have been born again and are not lost spiritually." Heath was not lost, but his soul was in spiritual warfare beyond a shadow of a doubt. After that day, Robert decided to get some help for Heath. He took Heath to an all-natural doctor in town, who gave Heath some medication to help with the depression. The doctor gave them two bottles and told Heath to take two pills in the morning and two before bed. A few weeks went by, and Ty, Robert's wife, noticed that both of the bottles were almost full. About the time Robert learned this, Heath pulled up in the driveway. Robert went out to Heath's truck with the bottles in hand, and said, "Son, you haven't been taking these, have you?" Heath slowly looked up at Robert and told him, almost in a whisper, "Dad, they're not going to help." Robert said he was at a loss and just kept thinking one day this would all blow over. The next red flag to go off was on Robert's birthday. Robert and Ty took a quick trip for Robert's birthday, and the first day they were gone Heath called Robert. Robert answered, and the first thing Heath said was, "Dad, are you sitting down?" Robert started to worry. Heath went on to tell him, "Please don't be mad at me, but I have killed all of Ty's flowers in her garden. Dad, please tell Ty not to be mad at me." Robert was confused and said, "Son, there's no way you could have killed them. We've only been gone a day." To get Heath's mind on something else, Robert also told Heath, "Bud, I want you to go into the gym behind the house and do the workout I have written down in there. Can you do that for me?" Heath replied, "Yes sir." Immediately when they hung up, Robert got on the phone with Heath's grandmother and asked if she would please check on Heath. As she pulled up in the driveway, Heath came out of the gym. She told Robert that Heath greeted her with a hug, and she asked Heath to show her the dead flowers. They walked around to the front of the house where the garden was, and he pointed and said, "See, they're all dead." She called Robert right then and told him,

"Robert, something is really wrong with Heath. The garden is as full of life and color as the day you left." When Robert heard this, he and Ty started home for Lubbock.

When they returned home, Robert did everything he could to get Heath out of the house and simply talk. But nothing seemed to be work. It was the morning of October 29, 2008, when Robert was about to head to work. Again to simply get Heath out of the house, Robert sat with him on a bench in the front yard and asked him if he would please mow the grass today. Heath quietly replied, "Yes sir." Robert told Heath he loved him, and he headed to work. As the day went on, Robert realized that he needed to pick up a check from the house, and around lunchtime he started home. He arrived home around 12:30 and noticed Heath's truck in the driveway, and the grass had not been mowed. Robert walked into the house and called for Heath, but he did not respond. Robert continued to walk through the house, and without realizing passed the room where Heath lay. He went upstairs, still calling for Heath, and finally came back down and walked into the room where Heath was. Robert immediately called 911, but it was too late. Heath was gone. A son, a grandson, a brother, and our best friend--gone. Seven years later, and it is still so hard to think about that day. We all gathered to celebrate the life of our loved one on November 1, 2008. Words cannot describe the love that was felt in the church that day. God was present as was Heath's family, who will forever be like a second family to me, and all of us men. I have lunch with Robert often, and I chat with Karen, his mother, and Amanda, his sister, on social media quite a bit. Not a single day goes by that I don't think about my dear friend. Robert Heath Stewart was born November 10, 1981, and made his exit from this life on October 29, 2008.

CHAPTER EIGHT

Picking Up The Pieces

AS THE YEARS go by, I will always think about my dear friend and miss him more than I can put into words. I will also always remember Heath's telling me, "Trust your gut, and do what your heart is leading you to do." That is exactly what I have done since the day I lost him. When I think back to the time I was battling my "demons," I thank God for bringing me through. Losing Heath opened up my heart even more to help as many people as I could. This lit a burning fire in my heart to take a passion God gave me and run with it. I was working a few different part-time jobs at this point in my life, but I knew I had to make a move in the direction of my true calling. I started building up my one-on-one clientele as a trainer so I could afford to do this full-time. I started holding boot camps at local parks and coaching a few classes a day at a small facility with one of my good friends Terell. The more I trained people, the more I fell in love with it because I was seeing people's lives change daily. Again, they would come in just wanting to lose extra weight or tone up, but I started noticing that it was doing much more. I saw men become better husbands and fathers, I saw high school kids change the direction of their lives, and I saw families become closer—all through this vehicle I used called CrossFit.

In October of 2009, almost a year after losing Heath, I was able to quit all of the part-time jobs and help others full-time. This was the biggest leap of faith I had ever taken, and by far the most rewarding! When I say rewarding, it may not have always been in the monetary sense of the word, but the fulfillment I got every single day from my "work" is something money cannot buy. It truly makes my heart happy to see others happy, and that is exactly what I started doing. My day would now start at 5:30 am and would not end until 6:30 pm. I coached classes all morning, did my personal training mid day, and finished my day with classes from 4:00 pm to 6:30 pm. This is not always an easy schedule to maintain, but when I literally saw lives changing before my eyes in the way I did, it was the fuel for my waking up daily. All my life I prayed to God asking what His will for my life was and what my true calling was. Day by day, week by week, I started to realize He had brought me to this point in my life, and I was never turning back! The money would be great some months, and others we would barely make it by. But I began to realize how amazing this life could be when I aligned myself with my true purpose. Our clientele base grew, as did my faith in what I was doing.

The years went by, and the business grew. In 2012 Monica and I were able to start looking for our first home to buy. This was beyond a dream come true. Every day when I finished coaching, she had already lined up the houses we were going to look at that evening. As tired as I may have been, I was more than enthusiastic to jump in the car and start our house hunt. I recall many days when Monica would be at work and as I looked for our new home, I would stop by Heath's gravesite just to tell him I missed him. In the midst of our beautiful life, I always wished my brother Heath could be there to share our joy. He always would say, "Trust your heart, Russell." It only seemed right that I let him know that I was doing just that. I know if my brother were here today, he would be so proud and cheer me on every step of the way. It never mattered how outlandish my dreams were; Heath always supported me 110 percent. He always told me, "Russell, I see the greatest of things in you, and you just have to find your heart's desire." On the days I would visit his grave, I always made it a point to tell him, "I found it, brother, and I am living it to the fullest."

During the month of May, Monica and I made our usual trips around Lubbock looking for our new home. Toward the end of the month, after a long day searching, we came to the final house on the list. It... was... perfect! We called the realtor and scheduled to meet him the next day. Monica and I were like kids the night before Christmas. He scheduled a meeting when I got off work, and we would see what was soon to become our new home. We showed up at the house the next day, and as our realtor opened the door, we knew. This was our next step in our lives, and we were more than ready. When we got to George's house that night, we prayed, "God, you know the desires of our hearts. Please open the doors to make this dream a reality." Between the money we earned by the end of the month and the money we set aside from tax season, we were ready to sign on our new home. Like most first time home buyers, I remember signing about a million papers, at 100 miles per hour. My heart was so full of joy, and I just thanked my God for bringing us to this point in our lives. Any time a major event takes place in my life, I think back to that moment in Big Spring when I almost took my own life. I become overwhelmed with a sense of love and purpose because I know I have special plans ahead of me, and these are all stepping-stones in my journey.

After six years of marriage, and after so many struggles, Monica and I moved into our very first home June 1, 2012! It was a bittersweet moment leaving George's home. After all, we had been through everything in his house together as a married couple. He witnessed all of our ups and downs and was always there to support us. For that we are eternally grateful.

I'll never forget on the final moving day, Monica and I sat down on our new sofa, in our new home, with hearts so full of gratitude. We looked around and became giddy about all we were going to fix up, and which room was going to be our first baby's room. And of course it was time to start planning the housewarming party. While Monica sorted out all of the details of the party, I had a major job to do. We were so blessed to find this beautiful home, but of course it wasn't perfect. The patio in the backyard was one of the biggest selling points, but the back yard itself needed a lot of work and love poured into it. I thought, "Surely I can handle such a job by myself." One of my many jobs after the golf business was landscaping with an old friend of mine. The problem with our new backyard was that it was nothing but goat heads. If you've ever been in West Texas for any length of time, I'm sure you know what I'm talking about. Goat heads are a type of sticker that when you step on them, you feel as if you stepped on a double-headed nail. Well, our back yard was covered in these stickers, so it was my mission to get rid of them. I got a price from my friend on 2,000 square feet of sod, and he said he could deliver it the next day. When I came home from work the next day and looked in my alley, there it was: eight pallets, and 2,000 square feet of grass, all ready for me to lay by myself. Dad called me, and said he and mom were coming by to see the house after we got everything in order. When they arrived, I was in the backyard laboring away at this seemingly endless task. Dad walked straight into the backyard and offered to help, and after I told him "No, pop, I got it," he started laying grass with me anyway. I was very adamant about dad's not helping because he was in no condition to be doing such manual labor. In previous years he undergone quadruple bypass surgery, with several stints put in his heart. As we continued working, I noticed that he became pale. As stubborn and hardheaded as he is, I forced him to sit in a chair and enjoy some of mom's iced tea. For two days I laid two square feet of grass at a time until 2,000 square feet of yard was covered. This task became a metaphor for my life. Throughout my life I had been in several situations where I could not see the end result, but I knew all I had to do was take the first step. Putting one foot in front of the other led to me back to Lubbock and finding my true calling. Putting one foot in front of the other led me to lose 40 pounds and become the man I knew was in me. Putting one foot in front of the other led me to my beautiful wife. Putting one foot in front of the other finally led US to this point in our lives. When I started the project in our backyard, it seemed impossible, but I realized after the fact that NOTHING is impossible!

About a month after the project was complete, and everything had its place in our home, we invited all of our dearest friends to celebrate with us. It was a beautiful summer night, and while we all enjoyed the company of one another, I could not help but wish my brother Heath was there. Again, losing Heath is also a daily reminder to be grateful for every moment I have with the ones whom I love. As the next couple of years passed, Monica and I did some traveling and simply enjoyed this new chapter together. I wake up every morning at 5 am and thank God for another breath of life and for every moment of each day. Like every married couple, life isn't always perfect and our marriage was put to the test on several occasions. Something I have failed to realize too often is that a relationship, especially marriage, is like every other aspect of life: you get out of it what you put into it. During the best time of our lives, things seemed to be going so well, but distractions came along and took my focus off of the beauty of my wife. So often I would put our relationship on the backburner, and due to that our marriage would suffer. Many times in the hardest of situations, instead of my pulling us together I pushed us further apart. After many financial struggles in our lives, and my putting work and other people before Monica, there were a few times when she wanted out. When I heard her cries one last time, and I was at a loss—much like I was in Big Spring—I picked up my Bible and began to read, and the first verse I opened up to was Psalm 34:17: "When the righteous cry out for help, the Lord hears and delivers them out of all their troubles." I told God that I was surrendering all of my personal desires to seek Him and to be the husband He called me to be. This became my daily prayer and my daily goal. I wanted to prove to my beautiful wife that I could lead her and our family the way she envisioned. There comes a time in everybody's life where they need to take a step back and reevaluate where their focus is. The more I did this, the more I was able to make daily goals in every aspect of my life. I wrote down on a piece of paper in my car all of my daily, monthly, and yearly goals. Number one of course was now to show my wife every day the love I have for her.

The more I focused on this and loved her with all my heart, the more she showed that love in return. As we went through our struggles together, we fell even deeper in love with one another. The more we fell in love with each other, the more we realized it was time for the next chapter in our lives. Remember my telling you the first night we met we even talked about what we wanted our firstborn child's name to be? Well, Monica came to me in November with a pregnancy test that read positive, and we started getting ready for our new addition! A few months later we found out we were having a baby boy, and his name would be what we agreed on eight years prior: Tristen Joe Butler. Eight years ago we sat on that swing in Heath's backyard and talked about naming our first son Tristen after the character in the movie, "Legends of the Fall." No more talking about it--that day was upon us! After Monica survived being dreadfully sick the first trimester, it was smooth sailing as we prepared for our baby boy to enter this world. We would stay up late at night setting up his room and picturing what it was going to be like. We would go into his room every night and pray blessings over him before he ever came along. If you have never had a baby, nothing can prepare you for that.

Nine months later on July 17, 2013, Tristen Joe Butler entered this world weighing eight pounds and six ounces. He was twenty-two inches long and absolutely beautiful! I held Monica's hand throughout the delivery, and the moment I heard my firstborn child cry, I had no words that could describe all of the emotions that went through me. Nothing can prepare you for that moment, but when it arrives there is NO better feeling on this Earth. I remember being so anxious when Monica went into

labor and all the way through delivery.
Once the doctor put my baby boy in my
arms, the world stood still. Every ounce of
love in my body poured out immediately
into him. I gave him his first bath, combed
his hair, and went to my amazing wife as
tears of joy streamed down both our faces.
We held each other for a moment while the
nurse was swaddling Tristen. The nurse
brought him over to his mama, and it was
time for the first feeding. In this moment,
I put my forehead to Monica's, and put my
hand on Tristen's head and thanked God
from the depths of my soul for bringing
me to this point in my life. I began to see
God more clearly in this moment than I
had since my encounter with Him in Big
Spring. My new daily prayer became, "Let
me seek Your face in all that I do. Help me
to be the father and husband You called
me to be. Shine through me in all that I do,
so my son will see You in me." A few days
later we were on our way home to begin
our new journey with our precious angel.
Being a father and a husband now gave me
even greater purpose to do all the things I
was called to do. My heart was overflowing
with love, and I wanted nothing more than

to share this with everyone I met. Every day my vision becomes more and more clear. After battling my demons and overcoming them, God put it in my heart to help others. That is my prayer every morning: "God, I thank You for all that is in my life. I thank You for bringing me to this point. Work through me, and allow me to touch as many lives as possible while on this Earth." In this life I realize we lose focus on the most beautiful of things, and the world can seem so dark. But we have to hold on to the smallest of things that bring joy, peace, and love. Every day is a gift, and we have to see it as such. From the moment I wake up in the morning until my eyes close for the night, I am eternally grateful for every minute of my life.

CHAPTER NINE

One Foot In Front Of The Other

I HAVE BEEN ON this Earth for thirty-three years, and I've probably learned some of life's lessons in the hardest ways, but I truly thank God for that. A friend once asked me if there was any moment in my life that I regret, and without hesitation my answer was, "Not one." This holds true to this day. Every step you take, whether it is the "right" or "wrong" step, is a valuable lesson, and only you have the power to learn from it and grow. Have I taken some wrong steps in my life? Absolutely! But without these steps, I would not be the man I am today and know how beautiful this life can truly be after seeing such darkness. Every choice you make shapes the outcome of your future. Looking back at my life I realize more and more every day how true this is. During my life after high school, I had no vision, I had no plan, and I was led like a leaf in the wind: no direction. I was guessing at every next step I would take instead of living with intention. All this did was to lead to a life of chaos and confusion. Like a lot of people in this world, I could have started seeking God and His intention for my life a lot sooner, but also, like a lot of people, I had to learn the hard way. Again, do I regret those times? No, I do not. Without a doubt I hate the Hell I had to go through in Big Spring, but without those experiences, I may not have come to know how much God truly loves me and wants to see my purpose fulfilled.

I'm here telling you my story so that maybe you hear it and relate. Maybe you can relate to me? Maybe you have lost a very special person in your life to suicide and can't quite put the pieces together. One of the main purposes of this book is to shed a light on the very dark subjects of depression and suicide. I am alive to tell you I have been there and have fought so many demons in my life. My dear friend Heath battled for so long. Depression is a very real and very disastrous experience. If you are in the midst of your battle, I am alive to tell you, "You can and you will overcome by the grace of God." If you are

the loved one of someone you feel might be
battling depression or suicidal thoughts,
start getting them help immediately. Talk
to them. Even when it seems impossible
to break through, your prayers and
encouragement are breaking those chains.
Speak loving affirmations to them, and
you will see the power of that love. If you
are the one battling, get out of your own
head, and begin to pray and talk to the One
who loves you the most. Confide also into
your loved ones, and let them know what's
going on. I know how dark it may seem,
but I promise there is so much beauty in
this life. Focus on something you love with
ALL of your heart, every day! Wake up, and
thank God for that one thing. You will start
to notice how much more you have to be
grateful for.

If you take anything away from my book,
take this: Every day you wake up there
is a battle for your heart, for your soul,
and even for your thoughts. Protect them
at all costs. Always seek the truth, love,
and beauty in all things. God surrounds
us in everything, and we just have to
acknowledge Him and be grateful for this
one life we have been given. Know that

God made each of us for a divine purpose, including you. Every day, wake up and put one foot in front of the other, and you WILL find that purpose. Once you find it, hold on to it and be relentless in pursuing it! Whatever good you desire in this life, that is what God instilled in you before you were even born. He says, "Ask and you shall receive. Knock and the door will be opened." Pray and meditate on His promises, and He is never failing. In the words of my dear friend, Heath Stewart...

"Always trust your gut, and do what your heart is leading you to do."

Made in the USA
Las Vegas, NV
05 October 2024